EVERYTHING THAT GLITTERS IS NOT GOLD

GALE HARRIS

Copyright © 2021 Gale Harris

ALL RIGHTS RESERVED. This book contains material protected under International and Federal Copyright Laws and Treaties. Any unauthorized reprint or use of this material is prohibited. No part of this book may be reproduced or transmitted in any form or by any means, electronic or mechanical, including photocopying, recording, or by any information storage and retrieval system without express written permission from the author/publisher.

Unless otherwise noted all Scripture, quotations are taken from the King James Version of the Bible, Thomas Nelson Bibles, copyright@1977, 1984, 2001 by Thomas Nelson, Inc. All rights reserved.

Scripture quotations marked TPT are from The Passion Translation®. Copyright © 2017, 2018, 2020 by Passion & Fire Ministries, Inc. Used by permission. All rights reserved. ThePassionTranslation.com.

Scripture quotations are taken from the Amplified® Bible (AMP), Copyright © 2015 by The Lockman Foundation. Used by permission. www.lockman.org

Book Cover Design: Prize Publishing House

Printed by: Prize Publishing House, LLC in the United States of America.

First printing edition 2021.

Prize Publishing House

P.O. Box 9856 Chesapeake, VA 23321

www.PrizePublishingHouse.com

ISBN (Paperback): 978-1-7379751-3-7

ISBN (E-Book): 978-1-7379751-4-4

Contents

Acknowledgments 4

Foreword 5

The Virtuous Woman (Proverbs 31) 6

Qualities of a Godly Man and Woman 7

Everything That Glitters Is Not Gold 9

Motive 11

Opportunity 12

Standards (Acts 4:13-20) 13

Insecurities 14

Overcoming Biases 16

Divine Relationships 18

God's Standard of Love (1 Corinthians 13:4a) 19

Purpose for Marriage 21

Loving Yourself 23

References 25

Acknowledgments

First, I must give honor to my Lord and Savior, Jesus Christ, who is first in my life. The God who makes the impossible possible at this age and stage of my life.

I would also like to acknowledge my leaders, Pastor Karl Wilkins and First Lady Jessica Wilkins, from "The Mount at Suffolk" in Suffolk, Virginia. I want to thank them for all their encouragement, love, and support.

I would also like to acknowledge Ms. Linda Perry-Clarke, who has been like a big sister and friend. I want to thank her for all of her encouragement and for allowing God to use her for His glory to tell me about Prize Publishing House.

Foreword

It has been a pleasure to know Gale Harris. She is an amazing gift to the body of Christ and such an inspiration to all she encounters. I have known Gale for a short time, and since then, we have developed a friendship that has grown into a partnership in the ministry.

Since becoming a part of our fellowship in 2019, I have watched her mature in the things of God and our Lord and Savior, Jesus Christ. She resides at the place where she displays a deep burden for souls, along with having a desire to share her life's experiences and knowledge of our Lord and Savior Jesus Christ.

I have witnessed her love for people that she shares as an educator. I sincerely appreciate the contributions that she continues to make in the lives of her colleagues and those she encounters. May all who read her book be forever blessed. Enjoy!

Pastor Karl Wilkins
"The Mount at Suffolk"

The Virtuous Woman (Proverbs 31)

The Word of God talks about the virtuous woman being one of strength and mighty valor! *"She is full of wealth and wisdom. The price paid for her was more significant than many jewels. Her husband has entrusted his heart to her, for she brings him the rich spoils of victory. Throughout her life, she brings him what is good and not evil. She searches out continually to possess that which is pure and righteous. She is a woman who delights in the work that she does with her hands. She speaks the truth and gives it to others"* (Proverbs 31:10-14, TPT). The price paid for her was the sacred blood of the Lamb of God, her bridegroom.

The virtuous bride will not bring disgrace to His name. Jesus will not be ashamed to display her to the world. Her prayer life overcomes her circumstances, even in a culture where darkness prevails. God says blessed is the man who finds a woman, for he finds a good thing.

Qualities of a Godly Man and Woman

A godly woman continually searches to find that which is pure and righteous. She has beauty, self-control and recognizes her worth as a woman. She takes care of herself. She knows when to help her husband and when to step back. "She is a helpmate and has the discernment to know when to help. She lives to the best of her abilities and is at peace with all men. She has value in Christ, makes a house favored, and is selected to be single or married" (Flowers, 2020).

A godly man is one committed to his relationship; he's a man who leads, values humility, and brings the goodness and favor of God in the relationship. He looks deep inside himself and can move past all obstacles, distractions, and temptations. He is determined to please God no matter what happens. "This man lifts, loves, and is a person of influence." He is vulnerable, which allows him to be emotional and open to physical and mental harm or attack. "He truly loves God, knows how to pray, and does whatever is necessary to stay in the presence of God. He is a man of vision, humble, teachable, and apologetic when wrong"(Flowers, 2020). Men and women of God are a blessing to everyone they come into contact with and serve.

Everything That Glitters Is Not Gold

I was born in the city of Norfolk, Virginia. I am the daughter of the late Mr. James Harris and Mrs. Alice Harris. During my early stages of development, I resided in the Lambert's Point section of Norfolk. My education started at the age of one when I had to learn to formulate speech. This training was conducted informally by my parents and grandparents. I consider the formal training I received an educational experience because it prepared me for life. I feel that any form of learning that helps one to prepare for living, whether negative or positive, is an educational experience. On the other hand, a noneducational experience is an experience that one has and learns nothing from.

I have learned during my time here on earth that everything is not what it appears to be. I was married for a short period, but it was someone that I should not have been married to in the first place. Would you please listen when your spouse's mom tells you not to marry her son because he is not responsible? Most women want to be loved and respected as a person. Some even give up what is valuable to them to accommodate the other person. There are so many women looking for Mr. Boaz. They think they have to dress a certain way or look a certain way, but that is far from the truth. I am here to tell young women and older women, just be yourself and wait on God if you truly want your Boaz. God will do it for you even at an older age. When I truly surrendered to the will of the Father, in less than thirty days, two to three men came, but I had to discern which one was the chosen one for me. Remember, the enemy sends counterfeits because he knows what you like too. Ladies, wait on God, and even though it should tarry, God will bring it to pass.

MOTIVE

Motive is a need or desire that causes a person to act differently (Motive, 1977). It could be for money, rewards, power, fame, or just wanting to be the best person they can be. But the only prize worth striving for should be our relationship with Jesus Christ. He is the sole and authentic way. We should be motivated by God every day. When God inspires us, He gives us purposeful motivation in abiding in Him as our Lord and personal Savior. He alone provides us with the reason to be who we are in Him. We as individuals have preconceived notions of what we think things should look like in a person. We tend to look at things on the surface rather than see them for who they really are. People and things can sometimes cause you to lose out on your greatest blessing. We should always consult God in every decision we make. He wants to be a part of the minor details of our lives.

Opportunity

Opportunity is a favorable juncture of circumstances that provides us rest and refreshment (Opportunity, 2021). God has given us this quiet time to attain a goal, a good position, chance, or prospect. It is an opportunity to start over again - a time to think about how we want to live our lives. It is a time to complete things and realize our hopes and dreams. When the pandemic has ended, people will run to find Christ because of all the things they have endured. Their perceptions of people, situations, and status in life are going to change. They are going to think differently and live a more abundant life. We are now looking at life through a stained-glass window, but all of that will change.

STANDARDS
(ACTS 4:13-20)

We should never apologize for having standards. However, a standard is not a standard unless you are willing to suffer for it. When you live by standards, you are called names, not invited to events, and told that you think you are better than other people. You are also sometimes considered a party pooper because you have standards. They will say you do not know how to have fun. To live by standards, we need to understand our "why." We live by standards because God calls us to live holy as God is holy.

God paid the ultimate sacrifice. He gave His only begotten son so that we could have the right to the tree of life. Standards put us in a position to avoid things that are not for us and to receive the blessings of God. We have to evaluate why we are doing the things we do. Why does my life seem to be at a standstill? Fasting trains us to hold onto our standards. It teaches us to substitute our will for God's will and apply it.

INSECURITIES

Standards set by other people we interact with, such as our family, friends, and peers, can cause insecurities. Insecurities develop when we start to compare ourselves to others. We can stop being insecure and build our self-esteem by affirming our values, prioritizing our needs, and embracing the fact that God created us in His image. The Creator wonderfully and fearfully made us. We can also build up our insecurities by keeping company with people we love and respect and those who love and respect us. We should not surround ourselves with people who cause us to feel insecure. We become insecure in our relationships with others because of our lack of love for ourselves, where we do not think that we deserve to be loved. Other times we are insecure because we believe that we will be a failure. Insecurities can also cause low self-esteem and poor images of ourselves when we do not feel attractive and confident. Insecurities can also create jealousy, which is when low self-esteem makes another person's successes or flaws seem more apparent than your own. Jealousy causes envy and creates greed, lust, and other negative desires. A jealous person can be sad, resentful, and covetous of someone else's possessions.

Overcoming Biases

Sometimes we have biases against people we do not know; we look at them and become judgmental. Preferences are what we perceive as being right or wrong for us. We have biases about size, shape, color, what a person drives, or even where they live. We sometimes use these biases to define a person. For example, we may equate skin color with the attitudes we think a person will have. We need to take the time to get to know the person. Our concept of what we thought or perceived often turns out to be different from what is true. I believe many biases started with rearing from our parents, then our preferences developed. I am so glad that God looks at the heart of a person and not the outward appearance. Looks can be very deceiving. We look at personal appearances and say they are attractive or handsome. When we get to know the heart of the person, we find out they have terrible depositions that sometimes make us wish we had never met or seen them.

Failure to deal with biases and unhealthy expectations can lead to abuse, which comes in many different forms. There is verbal abuse, physical abuse, mental abuse. Verbal abuse is when a person uses words to discourage or hurt you. Verbal abuse is just as bad, if not worse, than mental abuse. If a person constantly puts you down, saying that nobody else will want you if you leave them, that is verbal abuse. This type of abuse, if spoken continuously to a person, can have you questioning your sanity. We have to remember what God says about us. Only what God says really matters. God says that we are fearfully and wonderfully made in His image. It is not what people call us but what we answer to that matters.

Divine Relationships

In this season, God is putting divine couples together to get His work done for the kingdom and to fulfill the destinies of both persons. Every sacred relationship's purpose is the same, but not the process of bringing the two together. With some divine relationships, the two come together briefly, while in other sacred relationships, the two come together over a more extended period of time. I believe that we sometimes miss out on the better things of life because of our thinking. We have preconceived notions of what the spouse that God has for us should be. We should surrender our desires for God's desires because He knows what is best for us. God knows the heart of the person He chooses for us. Besides, God only desires the best for us.

God's Standard of Love (1 Corinthians 13:4a)

God's standard of love means that we decide to be kind in our tone, with our words, in our attitude, and with our actions towards another person. *"Love endures long and is patient and kind"* (1 Corinthians 13:4a, AMPC). A true disciple lives by God's standard and loves God's way. It is easy to love someone who treats you well, says what you want to hear, and loves you reciprocally. Endurance is to stay the course while experiencing something painful or difficult. Enduring long is choosing to trust God by allowing His word to be our final authority. Love is not an emotion; it is a decision Jesus made to love us by enduring the painful torture of the cross. Despite the betrayal and rejection of those closest to Him, Jesus loved according to God's standard. But it is not just about enduring; it is how we survive. God's standard is that, while we are waiting, we do so patiently by staying the course and trusting Him. Patience means that we are full of faith, despite the overwhelming hurt or confusion we may be experiencing. It is having the faith to fight against the spirit of strife, division, and disappointment instead of putting up walls. Patience means we refuse to be anxious and try to manipulate the situation on our behalf. Tolerance means that we allow the peace of God to rule in our hearts as we love. God's way, God's standard of loving people is that while we are enduring in our fight for unity, as well as being patient to trust God, we are also demonstrating kindness to the very one who has hurt us. Faith works by love. Our faith in God to heal, restore, and reconcile every situation works when we choose to endure, be patient, and be kind.

Purpose for Marriage

God's purpose for marriage was intimate companionship, rearing children, and space of mutual support for both husband and wife to fulfill their life callings. He created marriage because Adam was lonely and needed a helpmate (see Genesis 2:18). Once you get married, God no longer sees you as two separate people; He sees you as one and responds to both as one. God trains you for your spouse based on that individual's needs before He brings the two together. He knows the needs of the person that He is giving you.

Spouses should complement each other. When a woman is single, she has the covering of her father, but when she gets married, she is surrounded by her husband. Priorities should change when we say, "I Do." Our spouse should be before our career and everything else that we do. We are to be one with Christ as husband and wife. The ring is the symbol of marriage. When we make our vows, it is unto God, and He holds us accountable. The circle symbolizes the vows made to God, each other for the world to see. Even when we choose the wrong person, we cannot just get a divorce. You have to seek God to get a divorce. He says we can only get a divorce for infidelity or abuse.

Loving Yourself

Loving yourself means not comparing yourself to others. You are your own person with likes and differences. Realize that it is alright to say no when needed and learn to forgive yourself for past mistakes. Know that everyone is not going to like you. Recognize your talents and have fun positively using your God-given talents. Continue to wait on God to bring everything that He promised to pass. Keep the faith, and do not give up on your dreams. Believe that God will reward those who diligently seek Him and are called for His purpose. God is a man who cannot lie. If God gives a prophetic word, it will come to pass. It may take days, weeks, months, or even years, but God's words are truth and life. What He says will come to pass. While waiting, keep the faith and study God's word because this nourishes the body and soul. Believe that God is who He says He is because He is "The Great I Am." He may not come when you want Him, but He is always on time. What will be your decision? God gives us all free will to serve Him or not to serve Him. He will not force you to do anything that you do not wish to do. He is a total gentleman. God sees, listens, and hears everything that we do and say.

REFERENCES

1. Flowers, Jeff. [REDEFINED TV]. (2020, July 9). *Qualities of a Kingdom Man* [Video]. YouTube. https://www.youtube.com/watch?v=d8dlNPU3R2g

2. Flowers, Jeff. [REDEFINED TV]. (2020, July 21). *Qualities of a Kingdom Woman* [Video]. YouTube. https://www.youtube.com/watch?v=PJj8R8u026I

3. "Insecurities." "Opportunity." OxfordLanguages. Copyright © 2021 Oxford University Press. All rights reserved.

4. "Motive." *Webster's New Collegiate Dictionary.* (1977). Springfield.: Mass. G. & C. Merriam Co., pp. 106, 751, and 1299.

www.ingramcontent.com/pod-product-compliance
Lightning Source LLC
Chambersburg PA
CBHW062208100526
44589CB00014B/2008